Creative Writing Prompts for Kids Ages 8-12

Eleanor Thompson

Contents

Chapter 1

Adventure Awaits: Unlocking Your Creative Writing Powers

Picture holding a key that unlocks worlds where anything can happen. In these worlds, tiny dragons hide in your home, bicycles take flight, and mysteries unfold in the blink of an eye. This is the power you already hold at the tip of your pencil! With this book, you will learn to unlock this power to create new worlds and set out on wild adventures. Think of this book as your trusty travel sidekick, here to help lend you a hand along the way.

Finding inspiration to write a story can be hard. Sometimes, you have ideas but don't know where to start. This is something that all writers struggle with - even the authors of your favorite books. In this book, you will find all sorts of exciting story starters to get your imagination buzzing. Some of them are mysterious, some are totally wacky and silly, but they're all loads of fun! The best part? There are absolutely no rules! You can take your story anywhere you want, in any direction you choose. Don't worry about writing the "perfect" story or getting everything "right." Have fun and let your imagination soar!

Now, let's dive into what's waiting for you. There are eight chapters in this book packed with fun stuff for you to explore. Feel free to jump around and pick whatever catches your eye, or you can go through each chapter one by one. It's totally up to you! Here's a sneak peek at what you'll find:

Kicking off in the second chapter, "Tips to Help You Get Started," you'll find useful tips to kickstart your writing journey. This is where you'll learn how to build habits that make writing not just easy but downright fun!

In the third chapter, "Story Starters #1-20," you will find the first set of unique story starters. These are like the beginning spark of your very own adventure, from fantastical to funny!

Moving on to the fourth chapter, "How to Make Your Story's World Pop Off the Page," you'll learn how to build amazing places in your story. You'll get tips on how to make your story settings so real and exciting, they seem to jump right out of the book!

Next up is the fifth chapter, "Story Starters #21-40," where you'll find twenty "fill-in-the-blank" story starters. These are extra fun because you get to fill in the missing words and make the story totally your own!

Chapter six is all about "Bringing Characters to Life." It's like learning to make your very own story friends who laugh, cry, and have adventures with you. You'll discover how to make your characters jump off the page and come to life, ready to join you for tea or a space race!

Moving on to chapter seven, "Writing Prompt Questions #1-22," gear up for twenty-two wild writing quests. These aren't just any questions; they're like secret doors to worlds only you can imagine. Answer them yourself, or invent new characters to go exploring.

Last but not least, chapter eight, "Hooking Your Reader," is about helping you create your very own story starter hooks. It's like becoming a master storyteller yourself! Practice writing your own hooks right in the back of this book and share them with friends and family.

Chapter 2
Tips to Help You Get Started

Check out these tips to help you create a space for your creativity to thrive. You don't need to follow every tip here - select the tips that work best for you and your home.

1. **Find a Comfortable Place to Write:** Choose a spot where you feel relaxed and happy. This could be a cozy corner of your room, a sunny spot by the window, or a quiet space in the library. A comfortable place can help your imagination flow more freely.

2. **Create a Distraction-Free Zone**: Try to limit distractions in your writing area. If possible, keep toys, games, and electronics that aren't related to writing out of sight. This helps you stay focused on your stories.

3. **Make It Personal**: Decorate your writing space with things that inspire you. This could be posters of your favorite book characters, your own drawings, or anything that sparks your creativity.

4. **Invite Nature In**: If possible, choose a writing spot with a view of the outdoors. Looking at nature can boost your creativity and mood. Even a plant on your desk can have a positive effect!

5. **Use Music to Get in the Zone**: Some writers find that listening to music helps them get into the writing zone. You can create a playlist of your favorite tunes or try out instrumental music to inspire your stories.

6. **Keep a Writing Journal**: Have a special notebook where you jot down ideas, observations, and thoughts throughout the day. You never know when a random idea might turn into a great story!

7. **Surround Yourself with Books**: Being around books can inspire you to write. You can include a small shelf with your favorite books in your writing space or keep a stack of them on your desk.

8. **Share Your Space**: Sometimes, writing with friends can be fun and motivating. If you can, invite a friend over for a writing session. You can share ideas, give feedback, and encourage each other.

Chapter 3
Story Starters #1-20

STORY STARTER #1

Sam felt something hard under the cushion he was sitting on. He reached down and pulled out a dark blue hardcover book. The book did not have a title or any pictures on the cover. He opened to the first page. The first sentence was written in bold, neat handwriting. It said, 'Beware, for not all is as it seems at Elmswood Library.' A shiver of excitement ran through Sam. "Sam! Let's go!," his mom called. He tucked the book under his jacket. "Coming!" he replied.

_____

_____

_____

_____

_____

_____

_____

_____

_____

_____

_____

_____

_____

_____

_____

_____

_____

_____

_____

_____

_____

STORY STARTER #2

Jordan tiptoed down the hall and into the kitchen. He heard the noise again and shined his flashlight toward the kitchen counter. There, he saw a tiny dragon with a cookie in its mouth, looking just as surprised as he was.

_____

_____

_____

_____

_____

_____

_____

_____

_____

_____

_____

_____

_____

_____

_____

_____

_____

_____

_____

_____

_____

_____

STORY STARTER #3

Marion was just about to head inside when she heard an unfamiliar voice coming from her neighbor's yard. Curious, she peered through a hole in the fence. Marion gasped in disbelief. "This can't be real, can it?" she thought. She leaned in closer to get a better look.

_____
_____
_____
_____
_____
_____
_____
_____
_____
_____
_____
_____
_____
_____
_____
_____
_____
_____
_____
_____
_____
_____

STORY STARTER #4

Caroline stood back and admired her work. She couldn't believe she had finally done it! She looked around the old shed where she had been secretly working on her project. She couldn't wait to show her friends, but first she had to figure out how to get it out of the shed without anyone noticing.

STORY STARTER #5

Alex ran outside, excited to try out his brand-new bike. He hopped on and kicked off from the ground. The wheels turned smoothly as he began to peddle faster and faster. Suddenly, something felt strange. He looked down, shocked to find that the bike was no longer touching the ground. It was climbing higher and higher into the air.

_____

_____

_____

_____

_____

_____

_____

_____

_____

_____

_____

_____

_____

_____

_____

_____

_____

_____

_____

_____

STORY STARTER #6

Ava floated in the ocean, admiring the reflection of the bright sun twinkling on the waves. Suddenly, she heard a small, squeaky voice behind her say "Ava, I need your help." She spun around, surprised to see a small speckled seal with only its head peeking out of the water. She stared in shock. "Is this seal really talking to me?" she thought, "and how does it know my name?"

_____

_____

_____

_____

_____

_____

_____

_____

_____

_____

_____

_____

_____

_____

_____

_____

_____

_____

_____

_____

_____

_____

STORY STARTER #7

Chris stared in horror at the broken vase scattered in a million pieces on the floor. It was his mom's special vase, and she had forbidden him from ever touching it. He had never wanted to actually touch it until today when an odd glow coming from the vase caught his eye.

_____

_____

_____

_____

_____

_____

_____

_____

_____

_____

_____

_____

_____

_____

_____

_____

_____

_____

_____

_____

_____

_____

STORY STARTER #8

"I dare you to go in!" said Chris. "She won't do it," Bethany taunted, "she's too chicken." Sarah looked up at the abandoned house that sat at the edge of their neighborhood. The grass was almost as tall as she was and the windows were boarded up with old, cracked wood. "I'm no chicken!" she yelled back and walked up the creaky front steps of the house. As soon as she stepped inside, she knew that she had made a mistake.

_____
_____
_____
_____
_____
_____
_____
_____
_____
_____
_____
_____
_____
_____
_____
_____
_____
_____
_____
_____
_____
_____
_____

STORY STARTER #9

Mike watched the world whirl by as he sat across from his grandfather on the train. As the train entered the tunnel, his grandfather slipped him an old watch. Mike heard him whisper, "Set the watch to 12:01 pm when you want to come back." Then, everything went black.

_____

_____

_____

_____

_____

_____

_____

_____

_____

_____

_____

_____

_____

_____

_____

_____

_____

_____

_____

_____

_____

_____

STORY STARTER #10

Jess froze and looked around in disbelief. Her family had completely changed. Their voices were the same but their appearances were like nothing she had seen before. "Uhh, I better get to school," Jess said, wanting to leave as fast as possible. "Don't be silly, Jess" said the alien who sounded like her mother but most certainly could not be her mother. "You know today is the day that we travel back home to Mars."

_____

_____

_____

_____

_____

_____

_____

_____

_____

_____

_____

_____

_____

_____

_____

_____

_____

_____

_____

_____

_____

STORY STARTER #11

David was the most popular kid detective in his neighborhood. There wasn't a mystery that he couldn't solve. That is until one day, he introduced himself to the new neighbors next door. Bewildered, David found himself face-to-face with a boy who looked exactly like himself.

_____

_____

_____

_____

_____

_____

_____

_____

_____

_____

_____

_____

_____

_____

_____

_____

_____

_____

_____

_____

STORY STARTER #12

"It's getting late," Michelle said to her friends. "We should get back." They began walking back when they noticed something odd. The aquarium seemed quieter than usual. In fact, nobody was around. No humans, that is. They ran to the front gate and tried to push it open but it was locked.

_____

_____

_____

_____

_____

_____

_____

_____

_____

_____

_____

_____

_____

_____

_____

_____

_____

_____

_____

_____

_____

_____

_____

STORY STARTER #13

A small, silver button about the size of a dime had appeared exactly in the spot where Jeremiah had broken his arm. The button hadn't been there when the doctor removed his cast three days ago. "Why now?" he thought. Jeremiah didn't want to alarm his parents, so he decided to keep the button hidden at least for the time being. After all, he didn't even know what the button did - yet.

_____

_____

_____

_____

_____

_____

_____

_____

_____

_____

_____

_____

_____

_____

_____

_____

_____

_____

_____

_____

_____

STORY STARTER #14

Hazel was determined to win the annual baking contest. To do so, she planned to include a super secret ingredient in her pies. She knew it was a risk and that the ingredient was hard to find but she was desperate to win. "Besides, what's the worst that could happen?" she thought.

_____

_____

_____

_____

_____

_____

_____

_____

_____

_____

_____

_____

_____

_____

_____

_____

_____

_____

_____

_____

_____

_____

STORY STARTER #15

Luke watched from the front step of his aunt and uncle's house as his parents drove off. He felt like crying. He hated it here. There were clocks everywhere. On the walls, shelves, the floor, and even the couch. Each clock was set to a different time. Some didn't seem to work at all. "This place is so weird," he thought. Sensing his thoughts, his aunt said "Oh, don't mind the clocks. They're for our work. Don't touch them."

_____

_____

_____

_____

_____

_____

_____

_____

_____

_____

_____

_____

_____

_____

_____

_____

_____

_____

_____

_____

_____

_____

STORY STARTER #16

Ruby gasped when she read her name neatly printed in shiny black ink on the envelope. Excited, she tore open the envelope. She had been waiting for this letter for months.

_____

_____

_____

_____

_____

_____

_____

_____

_____

_____

_____

_____

_____

_____

_____

_____

_____

_____

_____

_____

_____

_____

_____

STORY STARTER #17

Carter peered into the incubator at the golden egg. He had found the egg weeks ago while playing in the backyard. He knew it must be something special, so he placed the egg in the incubator. Nobody knew about it except him and he intended to keep it that way. Today, he noticed that it had a tiny crack. "It's finally hatching," he whispered to himself.

_____

_____

_____

_____

_____

_____

_____

_____

_____

_____

_____

_____

_____

_____

_____

_____

_____

_____

_____

_____

_____

STORY STARTER #18

Margaret froze, the stage lights beating down on her. She had completely forgotten her lines. "This can't be happening," she thought. After all, she was the main character in the musical. How could she forget her lines? Everyone was staring at her and she could hear kids in the audience start to snicker. "I have to do something, and fast," she thought.

_____

_____

_____

_____

_____

_____

_____

_____

_____

_____

_____

_____

_____

_____

_____

_____

_____

_____

_____

_____

_____

STORY STARTER #19

Peter heard his mom's car door shut in the driveway. "Oh no," he thought. He looked down at the plate of crumbs. He couldn't believe that he had eaten all the cupcakes. His mom had spent hours the night before baking the cupcakes for his little sister's birthday party. He had intended to only eat one, but one turned into two, and two turned into three, and pretty soon, he'd eaten all the cupcakes. "What am I going to do?" he exclaimed to himself.

_____

_____

_____

_____

_____

_____

_____

_____

_____

_____

_____

_____

_____

_____

_____

_____

_____

_____

_____

_____

_____

_____

STORY STARTER #20

As Valerie sat up in bed, she noticed that something about her body felt strange. She looked down and gasped in horror: her hands and feet had switched places.

_____

_____

_____

_____

_____

_____

_____

_____

_____

_____

_____

_____

_____

_____

_____

_____

_____

_____

_____

_____

_____

_____

_____

Chapter 4
How to Make Your Story's World Pop Off the Page

Creating a vivid setting in your story is like drawing a colorful picture with your words. It helps your readers feel like they're stepping into your story. Think about your favorite stories, movies, and games. Where do they take place? How do those places make you feel?

When you write your own story, you get to create your own world with your own rules. It can be a place as familiar as your neighborhood or as wild as a land of dragons and magic. Maybe you dream up the future with cool gadgets or go way back in time. You can make your story happen anywhere!

Putting the world of your imagination on paper is like a fun puzzle. Here are some tips to make your story's places jump out and feel real. Try using a few tips in your stories. Have fun experimenting!

1. **Listen, Look, Smell, Touch, Taste**: Talk about what your characters can see, hear, smell, touch, and taste. For example, instead of saying "It was a sunny day," you could say, "The warm sunlight tickled my skin."

2. **Use Comparisons**: Make your setting easy to picture by comparing it to something. You could say, "The park was as quiet as a library," so your readers know it's very peaceful.

3. **Include Weather and Time:** Say if it's morning, night, sunny, or raining to help set the mood. Like, "The moon was high, and the wind whispered through the trees."

4. **Things That Move:** Describe things that are moving or changing in your setting. Leaves blowing in the wind, bustling crowds, or a flowing river can make your setting feel alive.

5. **Be Super Clear**: Use details to make your setting easy to see in your mind. Instead of just saying "flowers," say "big, bright sunflowers."

6. **Watch and Learn**: Look around where you are and think about how you'd tell a story about it. The more you practice, the better your story places will be!

Chapter 5
Story Starters #21-40
Fill-in-the-blank

STORY STARTER #21

"_____," Samantha yelled at Freddie. She couldn't believe this was happening. He promised never to tell anyone about the secret _____ she kept in her treehouse. He broke his promise and told _____ . Now, she couldn't keep _____ a secret any longer.

_____

_____

_____

_____

_____

_____

_____

_____

_____

_____

_____

_____

_____

_____

_____

_____

_____

_____

_____

_____

_____

_____

STORY STARTER #22

Adam rummaged through his closet and found _____. "Finally," he thought.

I can_____. He ran down the stairs and out the front door.

_____

_____

_____

_____

_____

_____

_____

_____

_____

_____

_____

_____

_____

_____

_____

_____

_____

_____

_____

_____

_____

_____

STORY STARTER #23

Thunder boomed and Jackie saw a flash of lightening through the window before everything went black. The power was out. As her eyes adjusted to the darkness, she saw a tiny _____ glowing in the corner of her room. She got up to investigate.

_____

_____

_____

_____

_____

_____

_____

_____

_____

_____

_____

_____

_____

_____

_____

_____

_____

_____

_____

_____

_____

_____

_____

STORY STARTER #24

The stray orange tabby cat meowed urgently at Sarah. "What's the matter?" she said to the cat. He swished his tail and walked a few steps forward. She walked behind him as he turned the corner into an alleyway. "This alley wasn't here yesterday," said Sarah. Puzzled, she looked down the alley and was shocked to see _____.

_____

_____

_____

_____

_____

_____

_____

_____

_____

_____

_____

_____

_____

_____

_____

_____

_____

_____

_____

_____

_____

_____

STORY STARTER #25

Max looked up at the old grandfather clock. This was no ordinary clock. Instead of 12 hours, it had 13 hours. Today was the one day of the year that it would strike 13 o'clock. When it did, Max would be able to _____ but only for one hour.

_____

_____

_____

_____

_____

_____

_____

_____

_____

_____

_____

_____

_____

_____

_____

_____

_____

_____

_____

_____

_____

_____

_____

STORY STARTER #26

Ariana put on her special protective sunglasses and looked up at the solar eclipse. The moon began to pass over the sun. Darkness covered the sky. "This is so cool!" Ariana exclaimed. Nobody answered. Ariana looked around her and noticed that all of the people that were with her on the town green were suddenly _____.

_____

_____

_____

_____

_____

_____

_____

_____

_____

_____

_____

_____

_____

_____

_____

_____

_____

_____

_____

_____

_____

_____

_____

STORY STARTER #27

This was Eric's first time at the beach since the ocean had completely disappeared overnight. It was a mystery that nobody could explain. Eric tightened the straps of his backpack. He knew he was going to be out on the sand flats for hours looking for _____. He knew it was a long shot but the reward for _____ was _____. Plus, he'd be famous.

_____

_____

_____

_____

_____

_____

_____

_____

_____

_____

_____

_____

_____

_____

_____

_____

_____

_____

_____

_____

_____

_____

_____

_____

STORY STARTER #28

It had been three weeks since Sadie found a pair of mysterious eyeglasses in the park. The glasses allowed her to see hidden messages written on the buildings around town. The messages seemed to be clues to a puzzle. The first clue said _____. She knew she was going to need help from _____ to solve this one.

_____

_____

_____

_____

_____

_____

_____

_____

_____

_____

_____

_____

_____

_____

_____

_____

_____

_____

_____

_____

_____

_____

_____

_____

STORY STARTER #29

For the past seven nights, Maria and Victor had been having the exact same dreams about
_____. They would both wake up with a jolt at the exact same time and
immediately send each text messages. "We need to figure out why we're both dreaming about
_____" Maria typed to Victor.

_____

_____

_____

_____

_____

_____

_____

_____

_____

_____

_____

_____

_____

_____

_____

_____

_____

_____

_____

_____

_____

_____

_____

STORY STARTER #30

Amy squinted, not sure if her eyes were playing tricks on her. She had been thumbing through an old family album for a school project when one of the photos caught her eye. It was a photo of her _____. Looking closely, she saw _____ move in the photo.

_____

_____

_____

_____

_____

_____

_____

_____

_____

_____

_____

_____

_____

_____

_____

_____

_____

_____

_____

_____

_____

_____

_____

STORY STARTER #31

On Josh's 12th birthday, he discovered that he had the superpower to change the weather with his mood. He felt _____ about this. He decided that he would use this power to _____. But things don't always go as planned.

_____

_____

_____

_____

_____

_____

_____

_____

_____

_____

_____

_____

_____

_____

_____

_____

_____

_____

_____

_____

_____

_____

STORY STARTER #32

Farah had always been scared of _____. Today, she knew she would have no choice but to face her fear. "How am I going to do this?" she thought anxiously.

_____

_____

_____

_____

_____

_____

_____

_____

_____

_____

_____

_____

_____

_____

_____

_____

_____

_____

_____

_____

_____

_____

_____

STORY STARTER #33

Ben became the most popular boy in town after inventing a new game called _____. All the kids in town gathered in the park to play _____. Today, Ben was going to add _____ to the game. He had no idea that this would cause _____.

_____

_____

_____

_____

_____

_____

_____

_____

_____

_____

_____

_____

_____

_____

_____

_____

_____

_____

_____

_____

_____

_____

STORY STARTER #34

Every Tuesday, Penelope woke up with the ability to speak any language for 24 hours. The catch? She could ONLY speak that language for 24 hours. Today she woke up and was able to speak _____. She groaned. This was going to be a problem because _____.

_____

_____

_____

_____

_____

_____

_____

_____

_____

_____

_____

_____

_____

_____

_____

_____

_____

_____

_____

_____

_____

_____

STORY STARTER #35

Colter was excited to go on his dream vacation to _____. He won the trip as first prize in an essay contest. He couldn't wait to _____. Little did he know that he would also find _____ and it would change his life forever.

_____

_____

_____

_____

_____

_____

_____

_____

_____

_____

_____

_____

_____

_____

_____

_____

_____

_____

_____

_____

_____

_____

STORY STARTER #36

Zoe ducked just as a laser beam shot over her head. She knew she shouldn't have travelled to the planet _____ on her own. Now she was stuck and forced to battle with _____.

_____

STORY STARTER #37

Every night, the statue of _____ in the town of _____ came to life.

Usually, it wasn't a problem but tonight the statue _____.

_____

_____

_____

_____

_____

_____

_____

_____

_____

_____

_____

_____

_____

_____

_____

_____

_____

_____

_____

_____

_____

_____

_____

STORY STARTER #38

Luca had only heard rumors about _____ living in the forest. He never expect-
ed to come face-to-face with one.

_____

_____

_____

_____

_____

_____

_____

_____

_____

_____

_____

_____

_____

_____

_____

_____

_____

_____

_____

_____

_____

_____

_____

STORY STARTER #39

Riley and Taylor had been allowed to camp in their backyard. They had spent the night playing _____. When they stepped out of their tent the next morning, they were surrounded by thick fog. As they walked through the fog, they realized they were no longer home. They were _____.

_____

_____

_____

_____

_____

_____

_____

_____

_____

_____

_____

_____

_____

_____

_____

_____

_____

_____

_____

_____

_____

_____

STORY STARTER #40

"_____," said Fiona's dog. Fiona was shocked. She couldn't believe that her dog could talk.

_____

_____

_____

_____

_____

_____

_____

_____

_____

_____

_____

_____

_____

_____

_____

_____

_____

_____

_____

_____

_____

_____

_____

_____

Chapter 6

Bringing Characters to Life

Characters are the heart of every story. They take us on fun adventures and teach us cool things along the way. Sometimes, they become like buddies we hang out with in our imagination. Without characters, there would be no story! Think about some of your favorite characters. What are they like? What makes them special? What makes you root for them?

Now, imagine you're an inventor, but instead of making gadgets, you're creating characters for your own story. You get to decide if your character is super brave, like a knight fighting dragons. Maybe they're the class clown who can make anyone laugh, even on a gloomy day. You can give them a crazy hairstyle, a secret talent, or even a little quirk- like they can only sleep with their socks on. And the best part? You can make them overcome big problems, learn from their mistakes, and grow stronger in the end. Let's dive into some tips that'll help you bring your characters to life.

1. **Give Your Character a Purpose:** Every character should have a reason to be in the story. Think about what your character wants or needs. This goal will drive their actions and decisions.

2. **Make Them Stand Out:** Give your character something special that sets them apart. It could be a hobby, a way of talking, a favorite item, or even a unique skill. This makes your character memorable.

3. **It's Okay to Be Imperfect:** Nobody's perfect, and your characters shouldn't be either. Having little quirks or things they're not good at makes them more real and interesting. Maybe they trip a lot, trust people too easily, or get mad quickly.

4. **Let Them Grow:** Characters should change over the course of your story. Maybe they learn something new or overcome a fear. This growth makes them feel alive to the reader.

5. **How They Speak:** The way your character speaks can show a lot about them. Maybe they use funny words, or they talk really fast when they're excited.

6. **Friends and Family:** Show how your character acts with others. It can show a lot about who they are, like if they're shy, funny, or really caring.

7. **Create a Backstory:** Imagine what has happened in your character's past. This can help explain why they behave the way they do. You don't have to write it all down in your story. Knowing it will help you understand your character better.

Chapter 7
Writing Prompt Questions #1-22

WRITING PROMPT #1

One day, you wake up to discover that all the adults have disappeared in your town. What is the first thing that you do?

_____

_____

_____

_____

_____

_____

_____

_____

_____

_____

_____

_____

_____

_____

_____

_____

_____

_____

_____

_____

_____

WRITING PROMPT #2

You win a trip to travel to any planet in the solar system. What planet do you choose to visit, and what do you discover there?

_____

_____

_____

_____

_____

_____

_____

_____

_____

_____

_____

_____

_____

_____

_____

_____

_____

_____

_____

_____

_____

_____

_____

_____

WRITING PROMPT #3

You return home after a trip only to find a family of raccoons has moved into your home. What happens?

_____

_____

_____

_____

_____

_____

_____

_____

_____

_____

_____

_____

_____

_____

_____

_____

_____

_____

_____

_____

_____

_____

_____

WRITING PROMPT #4

You discover a door in the back of your TV that allows you to climb in and become a part of any TV show, movie, or video game that you choose. What do you choose and what happens?

_____

_____

_____

_____

_____

_____

_____

_____

_____

_____

_____

_____

_____

_____

_____

_____

_____

_____

_____

_____

_____

_____

_____

WRITING PROMPT #5

You wake up to find that you have shrunken to the size of an ant. How do you react, and how do you navigate the world?

_____

_____

_____

_____

_____

_____

_____

_____

_____

_____

_____

_____

_____

_____

_____

_____

_____

_____

_____

_____

_____

_____

_____

WRITING PROMPT #6

You discover that sometimes your shadow detaches from you and lives its own life. One day, you decide to secretly follow your shadow. Where does it go, and what does it do? What do you learn along the way?

_____

_____

_____

_____

_____

_____

_____

_____

_____

_____

_____

_____

_____

_____

_____

_____

_____

_____

_____

_____

_____

_____

_____

WRITING PROMPT #7

Imagine you can have any animal in the world as a pet. What animal do you choose, and what is it like to have that animal as a pet?

_____

_____

_____

_____

_____

_____

_____

_____

_____

_____

_____

_____

_____

_____

_____

_____

_____

_____

_____

_____

_____

_____

WRITING PROMPT #8

A robot that looks like a robin shows up at your bedroom window carrying a message. What does the message say, and what do you do?

_____

_____

_____

_____

_____

_____

_____

_____

_____

_____

_____

_____

_____

_____

_____

_____

_____

_____

_____

_____

_____

_____

WRITING PROMPT #9

You're accepted into a school for kids with unusual abilities. What's your ability? Who do you meet at this school?

_____

_____

_____

_____

_____

_____

_____

_____

_____

_____

_____

_____

_____

_____

_____

_____

_____

_____

_____

_____

WRITING PROMPT #10

You find a journal that records tomorrow's events before they happen. How do you use it?

_____

_____

_____

_____

_____

_____

_____

_____

_____

_____

_____

_____

_____

_____

_____

_____

_____

_____

_____

_____

_____

_____

_____

WRITING PROMPT #11

You invent a machine that can control weather. How do you use the machine?

_____

_____

_____

_____

_____

_____

_____

_____

_____

_____

_____

_____

_____

_____

_____

_____

_____

_____

_____

_____

_____

_____

_____

WRITING PROMPT #12

Imagine if every time you sneezed, you were transported to a random place in the world.

_____

_____

_____

_____

_____

_____

_____

_____

_____

_____

_____

_____

_____

_____

_____

_____

_____

_____

_____

_____

_____

_____

_____

WRITING PROMPT #13

Imagine a world in which you could taste words. Describe the flavors of your favorite and least favorite words.

_____

_____

_____

_____

_____

_____

_____

_____

_____

_____

_____

_____

_____

_____

_____

_____

_____

_____

_____

_____

_____

_____

WRITING PROMPT #14

You are gifted a pair of sneakers that allow you to walk on walls and ceilings. Where do you go first?

_____

_____

_____

_____

_____

_____

_____

_____

_____

_____

_____

_____

_____

_____

_____

_____

_____

_____

_____

_____

_____

_____

_____

WRITING PROMPT #15

Create a story about a magical market that appears only at midnight and sells items from your dreams. What do you buy?

_____

_____

_____

_____

_____

_____

_____

_____

_____

_____

_____

_____

_____

_____

_____

_____

_____

_____

_____

_____

_____

_____

_____

_____

WRITING PROMPT #16

Write about a character who can travel through time by opening doors. Where do they go, and what do they change?

_____

_____

_____

_____

_____

_____

_____

_____

_____

_____

_____

_____

_____

_____

_____

_____

_____

_____

_____

_____

_____

_____

_____

WRITING PROMPT #17

Write about a character who can turn invisible in the rain. How do they use this power to uncover secrets or solve mysteries?

_____

_____

_____

_____

_____

_____

_____

_____

_____

_____

_____

_____

_____

_____

_____

_____

_____

_____

_____

_____

_____

WRITING PROMPT #18

Write about a character who can transform any object into a living creature for 24 hours. What do they transform first, and how does it change their day?

_____

_____

_____

_____

_____

_____

_____

_____

_____

_____

_____

_____

_____

_____

_____

_____

_____

_____

_____

_____

_____

_____

_____

_____

_____

WRITING PROMPT #19

Imagine a book that absorbs the emotions of its reader, changing its story based on how you feel. What story unfolds for you?

_____

_____

_____

_____

_____

_____

_____

_____

_____

_____

_____

_____

_____

_____

_____

_____

_____

_____

_____

_____

_____

_____

WRITING PROMPT #20

What if you had a magical compass that pointed you to your greatest fear? Would you follow it, and what would you find at the end?

_____

_____

_____

_____

_____

_____

_____

_____

_____

_____

_____

_____

_____

_____

_____

_____

_____

_____

_____

_____

_____

_____

_____

_____

WRITING PROMPT #21

Imagine a world where you can "download" experiences and skills directly into your brain. Which experience do you download first, and how does it affect you?

_____

_____

_____

_____

_____

_____

_____

_____

_____

_____

_____

_____

_____

_____

_____

_____

_____

_____

_____

_____

_____

_____

WRITING PROMPT #22

Imagine a world where you can send scents as messages. What scents do you send? Who do you send these scents to, and why?

_____

_____

_____

_____

_____

_____

_____

_____

_____

_____

_____

_____

_____

_____

_____

_____

_____

_____

_____

_____

_____

_____

_____

_____

Chapter 8
Hooking Your Reader

What makes a story exciting to read? Usually, it's the first few sentences that grab your attention. It's like when you go fishing. You want to catch a big, shiny fish, right? To do that, you need something special on your hook to grab a fish's attention. Like a wiggly worm or a shiny lure.

In writing stories, your readers are like those fish swimming in a big ocean of books. "Hooking your reader" is like using a shiny hook to catch a fish. You start your story with a really interesting sentence or idea. This grabs your reader's attention right away, just like a fish gets caught by a worm or lure.

But how do you hook your reader? There are lots of ways! Try these tips to write your own exciting and mysterious story starters. Flip to the lined pages in this section to experiment with different tricks. Feel free to circle back to the writing prompts to spark your imagination.

Here's a playful suggestion: trade your story starters with friends or family members. Take turns adding twists and turns to these tales. It's like passing a magic wand around, transforming ideas into captivating stories together!

1. **Jump Right into Action:** Make the first thing in your story something super exciting. Like a race, a funny accident, or a magical moment that makes your reader want to know what happens next.

2. **Introduce Your Character:** Show us someone really interesting or funny when your story starts. Maybe they're trying to solve a problem or they have a unique hobby.

3. **Let Your Characters Talk:** Start your story with characters talking to each other. This will make your readers feel like they are a part of the conversation in the story.

4. **Start with a Problem or Challenge:** Show a problem or challenge right at the start of the story. Your reader will want to keep reading to find out how your character solves the problem.

5. **Jump into a Different World:** Show what makes the setting unique or interesting. This can be a great hook for stories with fantasy or sci-fi elements.

6. **Start with a Dream or Memory:** Sometimes, a dream or memory can be a mysterious way to start a story. It could tell the reader something important about your characters or what's about to happen.

Dear Reader,

Thank you for choosing my workbook, Creative Writing Prompts for Kids Ages 8-12. As an independent publisher deeply passionate about fostering creativity in young minds, each page you've turned is designed to challenge, inspire, and unlock the boundless imagination within each child.

Your insights and experiences are incredibly valuable to me and to all parents and educators looking for meaningful content for their children.

By **scanning the QR code below** and **sharing your review,** you're not just offering feedback; you're becoming a part of a community that supports independent publishing and the creation of engaging, educational content for kids.

Your review has the power to **inspire more content**, **support independent publishing**, and **make a difference.**

Every thought, reflection, or story you share helps in crafting a world where creativity knows no bounds and every child feels empowered to tell their story.

With immense gratitude,

Eleanor Thompson

Scan the QR Code Below to Share Your Review!

Made in United States
Troutdale, OR
11/07/2024

24540540R00051